Catholicism

as a Corrupting Factor

Francesco Belfiore

ISBN-13: 978-1468010145
ISBN-10: 146801014X

Printed in the USA by CREATESPACE

Contents

iii

Introduction

In this book, I will attempt to describe, based on an already long-lasting personal experience, the way Catholicism is perceived by the large majority of Catholics, and the negative consequences that Catholicism, so perceived, exerts on the life of individuals and of society. This project excludes any "doctrinal" attempt to define the true meaning that, according to the Catholic doctrine, should be assigned to the various themes that will be considered, because such an attempt would interest a minority of Catholics, which I estimate is less than 4–5%, that is, those belonging to the class of intellectuals or, more exactly, to the class of intellectuals engaged in the field of human sciences (the *enlightened Catholics*); whereas the present book describes the way the majority of Catholics, which I believe is beyond 95–96%, perceives such themes and reacts to them.

It follows that this book is quite different from the books (on Medicine and Philosophy) that I have previously written, rich in quotations and bibliography. Here, the reader will only find a simple description of the way in which "common people", to which the large majority of Catholics belongs, receive and interpret some aspects of Catholicism. Thus, for instance, it would be inappropriate to attempt to discuss the meaning of "papal infallibility", its limits, its relationship with the collegial authority of the episcopacy or of the Ecumenical Council, etc., because, for the common people, there is only one simple truth: *the Pope is infallible.* Period. Referring to a totally different field, we could say that a similar consideration applies if we attempt to understand, for instance, the influence exerted by "sorcerers" on so many people. Thousands of people, belonging to various social economic and cultural classes, not only listen with conviction to the "advice" that sorcerers give them but also willingly pay a large amount of money for such a service. In order to understand this behavior, a careful *observation* of common people is sufficient; through observation, we can learn in which manner many people rationally "conceive" and emotionally "feel" the figure of the sorcerer and, consequently, how they adjust their behavior to cope with the suggestions given by the sorcerer. Engaging in *demonstrating* that the sorcerer's advice is deprived of any foundation and is only the result of charlatanism would be irrelevant to the discussion in hand. This book is not directed to *demonstrate* or *explain* what Catholicism actually is, but only to *observe* how it is perceived by most people.

The above considerations should not be regarded as meaning that the *enlightened Catholics* (who, as I mentioned above, constitute 4–5% of all Catholics), consist of the members of the high spheres of the Clergy and the scholars of the Catholic doctrine. Indeed, some positions, which I regard as unjustified (e.g., the alienation of women and the condemnation of any sexual act not directed to the procreation), are defended exactly by the high Clergy and by the Catholic doctrine. The minority of Catholics, made of the *enlightened Catholics*, is therefore present both among the Clergy or the scholars and among the mass of Catholics, and the same is true for the majority of Catholics, represented by the *non-enlightened Catholics*.

The title of this short book, *Catholicism as a Corrupting Factor*, requires an explanation, because the use of the term "corrupting" entails reference to some moral standard. The moral standard to which I refer is that of the public morality as conceived by the majority of people in most western democracies (which actually is morality as defined by the norms of the democratic constitutions and by the laws that derive from such norms). This moral standard is quite similar to that underlying the *Universal Declaration of Human Rights*, approved by the UN General Assembly in 1948.

Referring to an English book, which appeared a few years ago, in which Catholicism was criticized, a critic foresaw that it would have angered the Pope. I would like to expressly declare, instead, that I wish for nobody to get angry, but only to prompt some reflections on the negative effects that may be caused by some aspects of Catholicism as commonly conceived. Furthermore, I

would like to underline my deep appreciation of some of the founding values of Christianity. It would suffice to mention, for instance, the profound human meaning of love
toward one's neighbor, or the nobility of forgiveness, to become aware of the great moral
value of the Christian message, an issue
which cannot be the object of doubt or discussion. Referring to the practical aspects, it
will suffice to mention the loving and praiseworthy deeds of many parishes in the every-
day contact with their parishioners; or the
even more laudable deeds made by mission-
aries in various parts of the world. However,
I repeat, in this book I am not concerned
with the values of the Catholic or Christian
doctrine, nor with the deeds of priests; rather, I am concerned with the ways in which
the Catholic doctrine (and some aspects of
the behavior of the ecclesiastic hierarchy)
are perceived by the common people.

Another point that I would like to underline is that the negative consequences that,
in my opinion, are exercised by Catholicism
as perceived by the masses, are not unique
to Catholicism. Other branches of Christianity and other religions may be the cause of

similar or different negative consequences.

In the penultimate chapter of this short book, I will briefly discuss the issue whether those that I consider negative effects of Catholicism are indeed due entirely to Catholicism itself, or whether they are due, at least in part, to a natural or a culturally acquired inclination, which prompts some populations to embrace Catholicism; or, furthermore, whether there is a combined effect of both these factors. Finally, in the last chapter I will attempt to answer the question: Why Religion?

I hope that the reading of this book may serve as a stimulus for reflection that leads to a conception of Catholicism free from negative influences.

Chapter I—Infallibility of the Pope and Democracy

The Pope is infallible. His infallibility was defined in the *Decrees of the First Vatican Council* (issued by Pius IX, on July 18, 1870), entitled *"Aeterni Patris"*. It is defined, to be precise, in chapter IV of this document, which is devoted to the infallibility of the Roman Pontiff. The following lines reproduce the conclusive passage:

> Therefore, faithfully adhering to the tradition received from the beginning of the Christian faith, to the glory of God our saviour, for the exaltation of the catholic religion and for the salvation of the christian people, with the approval of the sacred council, we teach and define as a divinely revealed dogma that when the Roman pontiff speaks EX CATHEDRA, that is, when, in the exercise of his office as shepherd

7

and teacher of all Christians, in virtue of his supreme apostolic authority, he defines a doctrine concerning faith or morals to be held by the whole church, he possesses, by the divine assistance promised to him in blessed Peter, that infallibility which the divine Redeemer willed his church to enjoy in defining doctrine concerning faith or morals. Therefore, such definitions of the Roman pontiff are of themselves, and not by the consent of the church, irreformable. So then, should anyone, which God forbid, have the temerity to reject this definition of ours: let him be *anathema*. [see: Tanner (1990); also: Papal Encyclicals Online. http://www.papalencyclicals.net/Councils /ecum20.htm).

As I mentioned in the *Introduction*, it is of no use here to define the nature and the limits of papal infallibility (see: Powell 2009), because such a precise statement would not be taken in by the majority of the public of Catholics, which instead receives and understands the simple and efficacious notion that *the Pope is infallible*. Period.

The idea of papal infallibility, which pervades any aspect of the life of the Catholic community, is received from early childhood and is then progressively taken up and interiorized; it may act at a conscious or unconscious level and determines the habit of absolute and uncritical obedience to the decisions and commands of the "Chief", to which decisional infallibility and absolute power are recognized.

This conception of an infallible "Chief" who guides his followers acquires great force because it refers to a religious chief, who affirms that the source of his authority comes from God. This is, therefore, a conception that possesses a very strong moral, and therefore binding, force and a character of sacredness. Consequently, it becomes almost incvitable that the idea of the infallible chief is unconsciously extended from the religious sphere to the social sphere, thus bringing about an authoritarian conception, which becomes the sole recognized model of social organization, even when formally people adhere to a democratic conception (based, as it is known, on the respect of the norms and laws shared by the majority of citizens and that express the shared principles and values). In other words, an *authoritarian behavioral model* becomes prevalent.

9

The spreading of the authoritarian model is further favored by the way in which the Church is organized, that is, by the existence of the ecclesiastic hierarchy, which is perceived as an organization based on the principle of authority. [Even the simple priest, who occupies the lowest level in the hierarchy, exerts a modest and yet efficacious "power": the power of absolving of sins and then of removing any guilt].

From the above, it follows that in a democratic society a Catholic often has to face a dilemma: to adhere to the *authoritarian behavioral model*, which confers preeminence to the will of the "Chief" (that is, of the "powerful figure" of the moment) or to adhere to the *democratic behavioral model*, based on the respect of the "rules" (that is, norms, laws, rules, regulations, ordinances) decided by the majority of citizens by means of their representatives. Now, the "good" Catholic profoundly feels the fascination to obey the Chief, which necessarily entails disregarding the "rules", which are seen as something abstract, impersonal and almost evanescent. The result is that, under the appearance of a formal observance of the rules, there is the covered will of following the decisions (and therefore the interests) of the Chief of the moment. In this way, a conflict arises between the *authoritarian behavioral conception* (based on the decisions of the Chief) and the *democratic behavioral conception* (based on the rules shared by the majority of citizens).

Although the sufficiently long-lasting experience of the western world has demonstrated, in my opinion, the superiority of the democratic system over the authoritarian one, I think that some considerations on the negative aspect of the latter are not superfluous.

Previously, in 1861, J. S. Mill (in his *Considerations on Representative Government*) already warned against the false belief that an absolute but "eminent" or "enlightened" Chief or Leader may assure a good government. This is because the problems that the absolute Chief of a government should face and resolve (also true in the case of the Chief of the Catholic Church) are so may and so complex that he, however enlightened he may be, is forced to resort to the support of a group of collaborators who, in their turn, should all be "enlightened". It is apparent that this is an imaginary situation, which presupposes the existence of supermen, but which is impossible to be realized by real human beings.

Furthermore, there is another consideration worth of attention. Citizens who accept a government guided by an absolute Chief would be rather passive beings, who passively accept what the chief decides; they would be like little boys, that is, immature individuals, who need a Chief capable of guiding them (in the case of little boys, the role of guiding chief is exerted by the father, and/or the mother, and/or the teacher, etc.). Indeed, living under an authoritarian government does not help an individual to mature, that is, to exercise critical thinking and to actively participate in the social and political life. Conversely, it favors an indifference to the government of society and the acceptance of the results of the government's choices and actions, even if disappointing, because these results will be regarded as unavoidable consequences of natural facts. In a situation like this, the interest of most citizens becomes limited to their private life and directed to their material wealth and amusements, because the principles to be followed and the values to be recognized are defined by the Chief.

To be exact, one should remember that history teaches us that a government by an "enlightened Chief" may be acceptable and, according to some thinkers, even useful in exceptional situations, when there is a severe socio–political crisis and for a period strictly limited to the duration of the crisis itself; that is, the government by an "enlightened Chief" may only be accepted as an *exception* to the democratic rule. Instead, in the case of the Pope, the question concerns a Chief regarded as infallible and accepted as such not under exceptional situations but in a normal condition, that is, always, continuously, as long as the Catholic Church exists. And the "principle" of papal infallibility is imposed with so great a force and with so strong a pretension of an unconditional acceptance to justify the anathema for those who dare to doubt it. This is a conception that, clearly, contrasts the democratic conception of the government of a society.

13

How deeply the idea of papal infallibility is routed into the consciousness of Catholics is shown by their popular saying "Who do you think you are, the Pope?", which is often directed to those who show a firm conviction about the justness of their beliefs and attempt to impose their beliefs on others, rejecting any critique.

It should be underlined that the idea of an "infallible Chief", so widespread among Catholics, is completely absent in the mind of non-Catholic Christians. For the latter, there is not individual (whether belonging to the political or the religious sphere) who should be regarded as infallible, and hence non-criticizable. For the non-Catholic Christian, any human being should be judged without prejudices and with a critical approach, in order to be appreciated if and when he/she expresses merits or shows a praiseworthy behavior and to be censured if and when he/she expresses demerits or shows negative behavior. The non-Catholic Christian never renounces his/her inalienable right to criticize and to judge.

At this point, it is useful to mention some demonstrative examples that show the harmful effects exerted by the adoption of the authoritarian model.

(1) Within the *sphere of family life*, the authoritarian behavioral model supports the conception of the "father and master", according to which the father, as the chief of the family, is granted an almost absolute power, so that his decisions are respected without any discussion, because any critical attempt toward him would be perceived as a guilty offense to the authority of the father who is the master of the family.

(2) In the *social sphere*, the authoritarian behavioral model favors the submission to the will of the powerful individuals and the support of their interests, at the expense of those rules that require an equal treatment for all. Thus, for instance, in public tenders and in general in any public competition, instead of evaluating with impartiality the various tenderers or competitors, there is the trend to favor him who is perceived as a "powerful individual" (for political, or economical, or cultural reasons or for other motives) or those who defend the interests of the "powerful individuals". The same occurs in the various public institutions, including

15

universities. Progress in the academic career is often based more on the "weight" of the "powerful Master-Professor" who protects a candidate rather than on the real merits of the latter. Even those who hold public offices, instead of considering themselves as service-providers for citizens, consider themselves (and are considered by others!) as little "chiefs" who instead of providing services seem to lavish favors.

In short, the prevalence of respect toward powerful figures over the observance of the rules that assure impartial treatment favors the phenomenon of corruption in the public life.

(3) Even the *sphere of criminal activity* should be considered. Indeed, the myth of the infallible and authoritarian Chief also favors (even if it obviously does not determine) organized crime, as is typically with the mafia. Indeed, the appeal of the "powerful chief" attracts certain young people (especially if they are disorderly, poorly educated, and unemployed) to be irrationally prone to obey the commands of the mafia chief (or boss), even if this entails infringing the rules and laws in force. This is shown by the fact

that a well-known boss of mafia (Michele Greco), eventually sentenced to life imprisonment, was precisely nicknamed by his followers "the Pope".

(4) In the *political sphere*, it is clearly apparent that the prevalence of the *authoritarian behavioral model* (the cult of the "infallible chief") favors the acceptance, and even the desire, of an authoritarian policy, conceived as a policy in which the "weight" of the "great chief" prevails over the contents of the political program that is proposed. Thus, for an aspirant leader, what counts is to be perceived by the masses as a great and powerful "infallible leader"; this will allow him to obtain a passive assent by many (even most?) citizens, without any critical attitude or assumption of responsibility.

The spread of the authoritarian behavioral model is closely linked to the phenomenon of the excessive personalization of the political activity. When the various leaders who act in the political arena conceive themselves, and are conceived by citizens, as powerful and almost untouchable individuals, then the leaders are tempted to behave as special individuals who are above the law; and the citizens themselves may consider the leaders in a similar manner. In this way, a pillar of any democratic society is undermined: the principle of *equality before the law*. This leads to a contrast between the "powerful" politicians (or the politicians who regard themselves or are regarded as "powerful") and the Judiciary, at least in the political systems in which the Judiciary (as should always be the case) is really independent. Briefly, a contrast arises between the powers of the State, which necessarily entails a weakening of the democratic principles.

At this point, we may mention a further religious factor that confers authority and a special kind of "power" that, however, is not reserved to those who occupy the highest positions in the ecclesiastic hierarchy, but is extended to all the members of such hierarchy, including priests. The latter, indeed, because of their elevated number, acquire a preeminent role; here I refer to the absolution of sins. The authority to absolve of sins and to grant forgiveness, apart from the consequences that will be treated in chapter IV, confers a unique and special "power" to the priest, because a priest can absolve of sins, restore the cleanness of the conscience, and assure the salvation of the soul.

Chapter II—Miracles and the Anti-Scientific and Superstitious Tendency

Catholics are prompted to believe in the existence of "miracles", that is, phenomena that cannot be explained by means of the known scientific laws and which are regarded as due to a divine intervention (which should suspend or alter the natural laws). In reality, all claimed miracles of which we have enough knowledge (apart from those narrated or reported in writing) consist of phenomena that are, yes, rare but that may be explained without admitting a "divine" intervention. Thus, when considering the so-called miraculous recoveries, one should bear in mind that biological laws are not "exact" laws; they refer to "mean values", which are the most frequent; but there are also values that stand aside from mean values and are rarer the more they stand aside from the mean value. There are, then, or there may be rare phenomena whose features appear far, and even different, from the mean values. Thus, referring to any of the various "severe diseases" (a generic term that obviously refers to different clinical forms), we know that there are very rare instances of unexpected recovery. These unexpected recoveries cannot be regarded as the consequence of a miracle, because if we examine the frequency of miracles we would observe that it is inferior to that of the unexpected recoveries, that is, to that of the clinical instances of diseases with a very "atypical" course. Conversely, there exist instances, also rare, in which the course of a severe disease is exceptionally serious and rapid, causing the patient to die in a few days; an event, this too, unexpected. As confirmation that the so-called miracles are just rare instances (which as such stand aside from the more numerous cases that fall within the foreseen "range" of variation, based on observed cases), there is the fact that no ascertained "miracle" (excluding those just narrated or legendary) has concerned a phenomenon absolutely contrary to the laws of natural sciences, such as, for instance, the reappearance of a limb that had been amputated some years before.

Catholics, however, believe in miracles, and this belief often acquires features of superstition, at least of superstition understood in a positive sense. In fact, the superstitious person believes that there are some objects or some facts that bring good luck and other objects or facts that bring bad luck. A Catholic believes that there are some acts, like turning to one's patron Saint (conceived as a protector), that bring good luck, that is, allow to obtain miraculous results, otherwise impossible to realize. This means that Catholics adhere to a *superstitious behavioral model*. Superstition, however, is against rational and scientific mentality, free thinking, free feeling, and eventually against the intellectual and moral evolution of the world. This is shown by the absurd positions held by Catholics concerning questions as the *assisted reproductive technology, birth control,* etc. Not to speak of historical antiscientific positions held by the Catholic Church, like its contrast with the innovative ideas of Galileo Galilei.

It should be added that believing in miracles has another negative effect, as it induces the attempt to obtain results that are difficult to realize by normal means by resorting to a short cut, namely the invocation of a miracle (most often by turning to a patron Saint). This means that Catholics are prone to adopt a *miracle-based behavioral model*. Here, it becomes apparent that there is a close relationship between the believing in miracles and the cult of Saints (an issue treated in chapter VI), and that the miracle-based behavioral model has a corrupting effect. Indeed, it is evident that adhering to the miracle-based behavioral model prompts people to resort to the searching (and the hope) of a miracle in order to obtain the scopes and ends that are searched for in life, instead of founding one's expectations on one's own engagement and seriousness in study and work, on one's own decisional ability and initiative, associated to the taking on of responsibility.

We can quote many examples of the negative consequences of the miracle-based behavioral model. Thus, a student who must face an examination, instead of attempting to pass it by fully engaging himself in studying, trusts in a hypothetical miracle that he asks his patron Saint for. Likewise, the managers of an enterprise that have to face a public bidding, instead of attempting to win the competition by making the best offer (which should be the result of an efficient organization of their enterprise) hope in a miracle that allows them to obtain what they desire in a very quick and easy way.

In short, the consequences of the adoption of the superstitious and the miracle-based behavioral models are devastating both in the sphere of the private or individual life and in the sphere of the public life.

Chapter III—Rules that Cannot Be Followed and the Habit of Illegality

Catholics are asked to recognize and respect some rules that are actually almost impossible to observe. Of such rules, I mention here the obligation established by the 6th commandment. In the English version of the "Compendium of the Catechism of the Catholic Church" (2005), the 6th commandment, according to the "Traditional Catechetical Formula" is shown as follows: "You shall not commit adultery". However, it is then explained that:

> Although the biblical text of the Decalogue reads 'you shall not commit adultery' (*Exodus* 20:14), the Tradition of the Church comprehensively follows the moral teachings of the Old and New Testaments and considers the sixth commandment as encompassing all sins against chastity.

(*Compendium of the Catechism of the Catholic Church*, §493)

Moreover, it is established that:

Grave sins against chastity differ according to their object: adultery, masturbation, fornication, pornography, prostitution, rape, and homosexual acts. (*Compendium of the Catechism of the Catholic Church*, §492)

Of these prohibitions, I would like to underline those concerning masturbation and fornication. Bearing in mind that "fornication", according to the Merriam-Webster's Dictionary means "consensual sexual intercourse between two persons not married to each other", we could deduce that the 6th commandment prohibits any sexual act, be it practiced by a single person or with a person of the other sex other than the consort. But even during married life, any sexual act not directed to procreation is prohibited. This is shown by the following passage:

"Every action — for example, direct sterilization or contraception — is intrinsically immoral which (either in anticipation of the conjugal act, in its accomplishment or in the development of its natural consequences) proposes, as an end or as a means, to hinder procreation." (*Compendium of the Catechism of the Catholic Church*, §498)

From the above, it follows that the Catholic Church prohibits any sexual act not directed to procreation and, more generally, prescribes the obligation of pursuing the virtue of chastity. This, clearly, is a very difficult rule to follow, and it also appears as unjustified and irrational (of course, excluding any excess). In other words, this is a rule that all Catholics recognize (because it is a religious rule and, as such, is wanted by God), but that almost nobody observes (because it is almost impossible to observe). More exactly, it is impossible to observe for the majority of Catholics, that is, for about 95% of Catholics, to which I refer in this book.

The existence of rules which are at the same time recognized but unobserved has blighting consequences both on the way of *thinking* what a rule is and on the way of *feeling* the duty to observe it. Indeed, on the one hand, this state of affairs prompts one

29

to *think* that rules and laws are something theoretical, abstract, to be accepted only in principle, but without having a real impact on practical life, on concrete choices, on every-day behavior. On the other hand, this state of affairs makes people used to *not feeling* (or to feeling only weakly) the duty to observe rules and laws and to not feeling *remorse* (the voice of conscience) and *shame* (before others) for their violation. In other words, people become used to living by continuously ignoring and infringing rules and to getting accustomed to the *formal recognition* of rules associated to a substantial disownment of them. The majority of Catholics, therefore, when faced with a choice arising from an existing rule, end up by *thinking* (and *feeling*) that... in principle... from a theoretical standpoint... one should... but... in practice... everybody knows that... in this particular instance... In short, this leads to a *widespread habit of violating rules and laws*; and this is true not only for the laws of God but, all the more so, for the laws of human society. This means that the habit of violating rules leads to the practice of a *widespread acceptance of illegality*. All this occurs not only because of a warped way of *thinking* the rules (rational factor) but also because of a superficial way of *feeling* them (emotional factor). What follows is an easiness in violating rules without feeling remorse (voice of one own conscience) and without blushing with shame (before others)

The above situation is well depicted by the affirmation that Catholics "on earth recognize themselves as sinners" (*Compendium of the Catechism of the Catholic Church*, §165). Briefly, Catholics endorse the motto "we all are sinners". This expression means that *all* catholic human beings violate God's laws. If, then, violating God's laws is a common practice, shared by *all*, why should one feel ashamed for each infringing action? Why should we condemn those who violate the law? Do we not *all* violate it? If all this is transferred from the religious to the socio-political sphere, and applied to the laws of a democratic State, what ensues is a condition of *widespread illegality*.

Some examples may be useful to illustrate how extensive the variety of consequences that can be caused by the widespread habit of illegality is.

Let us begin by considering *the sphere of the family life*, and in particular the way in which adolescents and young people receive parents' advice; and let us refer to that advice that adolescents and young people recognize as *just*. Of such advice, let us consider, for instance, the one of not to drinking and driving. Most young people, faced with the rule that forbids driving in the state of drunkenness, recognize that this is a just rule. Yet, when, late at night, one is in a disco (and is aware that to go back home he/she has to drive) starts to drink and drinks a lot; then he/she leaves the disco while being slightly drunk, together with friends and girls. At this point, the habit of illegality intervenes and, perhaps unconsciously, one considers the prohibition of driving while in a state of drunkenness as an abstract principle, a theoretical statement, a rule that *should* be followed but that... in practice... everybody knows... in this particular situation... together with friends and girls...; thus, one ends up transgressing.

In *the sphere of social life*, we could refer to various kinds of examples. Thus, when participating in a public tender, the rules that establish the criteria and procedures for an honest and objective evaluation of the various competitors are regarded as something of abstract, as theoretical principles that do not resist the pressure of concrete interests, the call of friendship, the wish to favor the "most powerful" participant; and, most often, these factors end up by prevailing on the rules. Something similar occurs in various institutions, namely, public offices, universities, etc. Most or, at least, many "public officials" often favor personal interests, or the interests of relatives, or of friends, or of "powerful individuals", at the expense of the general interests and the legitimate interests of the single individual, as defined by the laws and rules in force. A typical example is given by universities, in which senior professors, when having to select new researchers and professors, "conceive" and "feel" the rule of evaluating the candidates based on their merits as something of theoretical, abstract, and vague, which does not stand up to the tempting prospect of bestowing positive assessments directed to satisfy his own ambition (by supporting his pupils), or to favor relatives and friends, or to meet the interests of the "important persons".

A phenomenon that exerts far-reaching effects is represented by tax evasion, a scourge that, to a various extent, afflicts several countries. The payment of taxes is prescribed by the law, and is a duty that any (adult) citizen should recognize as an important one, because it fulfillment is required to make the functioning of society possible; in particular, it allows that the various social services are provided to citizens. However, even in this instance, *the rule* prescribing the payment of taxes is perceived as a theoretical rule, an abstract principle, based on which one, theoretically, ought... but in practice... everybody knows that... in this particular situation... The result of this is a high rate of tax evasion, which compromises the correct functioning of society. This is because many people, used to living by continuously violating the rules, ignore the tax laws without the awareness of the severe illegality (and hence immorality) of their behavior, neither at a rational level (they *think* that rules are valid in theory, but in practice...) nor at an emotional level (they *feel* that to violate rules in the practical life is something common, allowed, and even licit). It is not by chance that one of the highest rates of tax evasion occurs in Italy, a Catholic country that houses the highest hierarchies of the Catholic Church, whereas in countries where the population is prevalently non-Catholic, such as Great Britain or Sweden, the rate of tax evasion is much lower.

In the *political sphere*, the habit of violating rules manifests itself by a sort of leniency toward those who show a corrupt behavior. Indeed, once the understanding of the seriousness of violating the rules is lost, the corrupt person who, by definition, is someone who profits and obtains power and even prestige by violating the laws, is often admired for the position he has reached, which makes him a person who counts. At the same time, the illegal means that he has adopted vanish or even disappear into the dark maze of the conscience used to illegality of those who know him, who go round with him, and who often support him. On this ground, it is possible to explain why several or many individuals already condemned, or under trial, for severe crimes succeed in occupying elective positions in public institutions (a typical example: the position of a member of parliament), being elected by numerous citizens.

A phenomenon perfectly symmetric to that described above is represented by the non-appreciation, or even by the intolerance and/or derision, which is expressed toward those who respect the laws and promote the culture of legality. This is because, once the sense of the value of legality is lost, those who defend legality are perceived as captious individuals who pretend to impose a system of absurd bonds and obstacles to the free pursuing of one's particular interests, accomplished without caring for the negative consequences on the "common good", the latter being perceived (like the rules that assure its realization) as something abstract, vague, and vanishing.

On the grounds of the above, it becomes clear that the prevalence of the habit of illegality favors the forming of a disordered and corrupt society; a society in which the failure to respect the rules leads not only to a moral decay but also to a restraint on the economic and civil development, for which the observance of rules and laws represents the necessary presupposition.

Chapter IV—Easy Forgiveness

As it is known, "the Forgiveness of Sins" consists of the forgiveness that God grants the sinner when the latter, who has violated God's law, sincerely repents his/her sins and goes to confession; that is, when the sinner, by going to confession, recognizes his/her sin and shows regret having committed it and the sincere intention of not committing it again. In the *Compendium of the Catechism of the Catholic Church*, it is said that "The confession of serious sins is the only ordinary way to obtain forgiveness" (§304).

I would like to underline at once that forgiveness, when there is sincere repentance, is an act that expresses great moral sensibility either in he/she who forgives (who in this way shows profound goodness of heart and human sympathy) and in he/she who asks and obtains the forgiveness (whose soul, through the confession and the renounce to sin again, expresses a renewed trend and a revived aspiration toward the good). An act of so high a meaning is, by its nature, rare, in the sense that it takes place in the rare instances in which a person commits a serious sin and then sincerely repents it. For this reason, things are different when forgiveness is asked and granted repeatedly and frequently, because the continuous repetition of the sin indicates that there has not been, and there is not, a sincere repentance. In these instances, what actually occurs is that an act so human and noble, as forgiveness, is devalued and reduced to the farce of forgiveness.

An example of true repentance and of true forgiveness, high and noble, is found in the conversion of *L'Innominato* ("The Unnamed") as described in the great novel *I Promessi Sposi* ("The Betrothed") by A. Manzoni (1840-42), a conversion prompted by the figure of a true Christian, predisposed to human sympathy and forgiveness: the Cardinal F. Borromeo. This is the case of a great sinner who, at a certain point of his life, moved by some particular events, experiences a profound crisis of conscience, a true repentance, which leads him to turn to Cardinal Borromeo, who receives him with open arms. A noble and touching event.

Yet in the life of most Catholics, things are quite different. In the *Compendium of the Catechism of the Catholic Church* (2005), it is said that "Each of the faithful who has reached the age of discretion is bound to confess his or her mortal sins *at least* once a year" (§305; italics added). If we assume that reaching "the age of discretion" means to come of age, which is thought to occur at about the age of 18, and considering that in the Western World the mean life expectancy is around the age of 80, it follows that every Catholic should confess his serious or mortal sins *at least* sixty-two times during his life. However, sixty-two should be the minimum number of sin-repentance-forgiveness episodes, as indicated by the words "at least" used in the *Compendium of the Catechism*, quoted above. We might therefore suppose that most Catholics experience the episodes of sin-repentance-forgiveness approximately two times a year, which corresponds to about one hundred and twenty-four of such episodes during their life. And certainly for many Catholics such episodes will be even more numerous. All of this means that in the life of Catholics *easy forgiveness* has a great importance.

Easy forgiveness is linked to the easy inobservance of rules and the habit of illegality (see the preceding chapter). This is because he who is used to not observing the rules, and therefore has the habit of illegality, behaves in this way also because he expects that, if and when his wrong actions become known, he will be easily forgiven. One could ask: forgiven by whom? The answer might be that, if forgiveness if easily given by God (through His ministers) for the violation of the divine laws, even more so it should be given by humans for the violation of human laws; that is, forgiveness should be given by family members, relatives, friends, acquaintances and, ultimately, by the entire society. It could be said that the habit of not observing the law and the expectance or even the pretension of easy forgiveness are two aspects of the same phenomenon (or two sides of the same coin); the first aspect concerns

42

the subjective or personal component of the phenomenon (I ignore the rules because I do not "understand" or "feel" their value), whereas the second aspect concerns the objective or impersonal component (almost everyone ignores the rules and hence, if some people know my incorrectness, they will easily forgive me).

This way of thinking and feeling is associated with a more or less pronounced lack of assumption of responsibility, because the sense of responsibility consists in having the awareness of the consequences of one's own actions and, therefore, in recognizing one's own guilt when one violates a rule, guilt that can only be forgiven after a sincere repentance.

Easy forgiveness, which I have discussed above, is the one granted, as already mentioned, by relatives, friends and acquaintances and even by all the community. This is so until the incorrect actions remain limited to the private sphere and do not become *publicly demonstrable*. In these instances, therefore, we are dealing with a forgiveness of private-moral nature. Yet private-moral forgiveness does not also entail a public-

moral (i.e., legal) forgiveness; that is, a forgiveness granted by the public institutions.
The law, in fact, except in rare instances
concerning those underage, does not forgive.
This leads to the necessity of hiding, or better, of making publicly non-demonstrable,
the violations of the rules (here we are talk-
ing of the laws in force) to which the Catholic is used. With time, by practicing the "art"
of making publicly non-demonstrable the violation of the laws, many people acquire an
experience and even skill in this ignoble art,
so that the person who practices it assumes
an attitude of self-confidence and of arrogance, which may even go so far as to become impudence. Shortly, getting into the
habit of being repeatedly and continuously
forgiven is something that does not remain
limited to the sphere of religious or moral
precepts, but becomes a psychic aptitude
that also extends to the laws of the State.
Shortly, we could say that easy forgiveness
leads to a behavioral model that we could
define as an *immoral behavioral model.*

The consequences of easy forgiveness
(easily granted and therefore expected and
almost pretended) are serious and of various

nature. We could give several examples.

Thus, the Catholic tax evader is a citizen who not only lightly violates the law (because, as I mentioned in chapter III, he assigns little weight to the observance of the laws and is used to violating them), but he expects and in practice pretends that, once his illegal behavior becomes known, he should be forgiven; that is, that his wrong should be completely wiped out.

Likewise, when, in public tenders or competitions, those who decide who the winner is, instead of considering the true merits of the competitors, adopt criteria of patronage (by favoring relatives, friends, or those recommended by "powerful individuals"), do this being certain (and almost pretending) of being forgiven. For this reason, illegal behavior is often not kept hidden, and sometimes it is even shown off as a token of "importance". Moreover, he who takes an incorrect decision is often pleased, inasmuch as he not only obtains the forgiveness for his incorrect behavior, but he increases his prestige, that is, he is regarded as someone who "counts".

In the political sphere, often a party leader or a member of the Executive or of Parliament, who has committed illegal actions (corruption, bribery, etc.) that have become known by some or many people, pretends and obtains the forgiveness from his supporters; this is shown by the instances in which corrupted leaders are re-elected. Any possible expression or attitude of condemnation is often regarded by the corrupted politician almost as a hostile action toward him, an action of enmity, because he, perhaps unconsciously, asks himself: if anybody is forgiven, why should you refuse to forgive me and judge me as guilty? Why this "unjust" treatment?

I would like to close this chapter by quoting an old Sicilian saying, which expresses, in a concise but efficacious way, the expectance-pretension of an easy forgiveness for any bad conduct. Reporting this saying literally is impossible, without using coarse words. So I will translate it as follows: "Refrain not from immoral acting / for our Lord forgives anything"!

Chapter V—Alienation of Women and Male-Chauvinism

In the organization of the Catholic Church, nothing is as evident as the exclusion of women from the key roles: women cannot hold the role of Pope, Cardinal, Bishop, or Priest. Of course, women are allowed to exert some functions, even of remarkable importance, in the Catholic world; it suffices to mention the work of nuns, or the cult of the numerous Saints, not to speak of the worship of the Virgin Mary (and the importance of her historical role). However, ascribing great importance to women does not mean to recognize equal dignity and rights between women and men. In the patriarchal (and anti-democratic) societies of the past centuries (until the first decades of the 20th century) women were denied the right to vote and the right to possess property, their access to education and culture was much limited, etc. Yet, a head of family of those times would have not hesitated to recognize that women play an important role in the life of the family and of society, because women beget children, care for their education, look after the home, etc. Yet, this does not annul the fact that women were only allowed to hold lower rank positions. If someone had asked such heads of family to grant women equality of rights, they would have opposed a resolute (and almost furious) "NO". And "no" has always been the answer of the Popes to the requests emerging from society for equality between women and men within the organization of the Church. Pope Benedict XVI, in his book-interview *Luce del Mondo* ("Light of the World"), made with the German reporter Peter Seewald (Libreria Editrice Vaticana, 2010), has confirmed "no" to the access of women to priesthood, and has affirmed that the Church "cannot" allow women to become priests because this is "the will of the Lord... to which we cling". With this statement, Benedict XVI, perhaps involuntarily, has ratified in a definitive manner that the access to priesthood must be forbidden to women because, he says, this is the will of the Lord; and the will of the Lord cannot be contradicted, either now or in the future, because it has eternal validity. This means that women cannot even hope that in the future the Church may change its attitude towards them.

In this way, the inferiority of women in respect to men is definitely ratified.

Once the Catholic has, so to speak, interiorized into the subconscious that women can only play a secondary or subordinate role (auxiliary to that of men), and that, therefore, the access to apical or most important positions is precluded to them, he will act consequently in all aspects of his activity and in all sectors of society; that is, a *male-chauvinist behavioral model* will be adopted. The results of this are well evident in those societies in which Catholicism is more widespread and more strongly felt, or where the influence of the Catholic hierarchies is more pressing such as Italy.

Thus, it happens that the percentage of women in the boards of directors of the major economic enterprises is very low; that the number of women in the most influential positions in Universities is always lower than that of men; that the women elected to public offices are always less in number compared to men; etc.

In Italy, a study carried out by the Observatory of a primary university institution has shown that women hold 37% of the lower positions and 13% of the higher (managerial) positions. Some difficulty for women in accessing the highest degree of professional careers, unfortunately, is a datum observable also in other European countries, even if with significant differences between the various countries, differences whose analysis is clearly outside the scope of this book.

For the same reason, it is no wonder that salary or earning received by women is often rather lower than that received by men, under the same kind of work and duties.

Chapter VI—The Cult of Saints as "Protectors"

In the catholic world, the cult of Saints is very widespread. Almost any Catholic has his "patron Saint", and the same is true for almost every town and even for most countries. The patron Saint is the Saint to which one is a devotee. The *devotion to the patron Saint* is grounded on two beliefs. *Firstly*, Catholics believe that Saints can "grant graces" or "make miracles"; these, indeed, are improper expressions to mean that, by the intercession of Saints, God grants the grace (or effects the miracle), because graces or miracles are always the work of God — but, as I have already mentioned, most Catholics do not understood the more precise information. *Secondly*, Catholics believe that any patron Saint grants his devotees graces or miracles in exchange for a small sacrifice (the act of renouncing something or of doing something that entails some discomfort or suffering), or in exchange of some gift or donation made to the statue of the patron Saint or to the Church consecrated to the Saint, or to some religious institution or association again consecrated to such a Saint, or other similar donations.

The practice of obtaining what one desires (for himself or for those whom he cares) through gifts or donations to the patron Saint is quite widespread among Catholics, and may concern situations of different meaning.

A first situation is that of a Catholic who offers a gift or makes a donation to his/her patron Saint in order to spare a loved-one from grief or suffering that appears as probable and imminent. A typical example is that of a mother who, having learned that her young son has an incurable disease, turns to her Saint for a miracle (or a grace) to heal her son in exchange for a gift or donation, in the form of a jewel or of money, for the Church consecrated to that Saint. [I am aware that the term "in exchange" that I have just used would be questioned by a scholar of the Catholic doctrine, but this, as I have already repeatedly said, is irrelevant to my discourse, which is directed to describe what the large majority of Catholics thinks and feels]. Now, the hypothetical mother to which I referred in the above example is worthy of admiration, since she has expressed her profound maternal love and faced a sacrifice in order to save her own son. Of course, one could object that such a mother shows a very poor conception of "her" Saint, who "grants the miracle" of saving the life of the incurable young son (actually, intercedes with God to obtain that God makes the miracle) only if that mother offers a gift or makes a donation, otherwise the Saint would leave the young boy sick without doing anything. But, I once again repeat, to thoroughly analyze this aspect of the behavior of that mother is not useful for our discourse; whichever the conception of that mother concerning her Saint, she has accomplished an act of profound maternal love. Not much different is the case of he who asks the Saint a miracle for himself, such as the miracle of recovering from a serious disease. In this instance too, one is dealing with an understandable and acceptable behavior, which does not damage anyone while leading to a benefit for he who asked for the miracle.

However, a second and very common situation exists, which has quite a different meaning. This is the case of a Catholic who offers a gift to the Saint to whom he is devout in order to ask that himself, or a person for whom he cares, *may obtain what one honestly and legally could not obtain (that is, may reach illegal goals)*. The example might be that of a mother who, knowing that her son has to face a public exam for a limited number of positions (let us say, ten), and knowing that her son has a low possibility to pass the test due to his poor preparation, turns to "her" patron Saint asking him that her son passes the test, that is, is ranked among the first ten candidates, *in exchange* of a gift *x*. Before analyzing the behavior of this mother, we should make a distinction. If this mother asks the Saint that those who should evaluate the candidates act correctly, assigning the marks based on the true merits of the candidates (without favoring anyone), this mother deserves admiration. She, in fact, asks that those who evaluate the candidates act in a correct and honest way, which is a very legitimate request. Things are different if that mother asks her Saint that her son is included (despite not deserving so) within the first ten candidates, which necessarily will only occur *at the expense of another competitor who deserves to pass the exam.* [The mechanism through which this miracle may take place does not matter. It could occur because by chance the tests cover the only few notions that the son of that mother knows; or because those who evaluate the competitors make some mistake; or other]. This mother, then, asks for the intervention of her patron Saint to obtain, by any mechanism, that the competition occurs in such a way as to favor her son, who does not deserve so, and to damage one of the other candidates, who deserves so. Here, judgment must necessarily be entirely negative. Indeed, the case just mentioned represents the exemplification of an extremely common behavioral model among Catholics, consisting in *obtaining advantages by paying a bribe to a "powerful person" in order to violate the laws* (referring to the above example, here the "powerful person" substitutes the "patron Saint"). Otherwise stated, this behavioral model consists in making the will of a "powerful individual" prevail over the laws. This is an *anti-legalistic and corrupting behavioral model*, whose widespread adoption has devastating social effects. Here, one could repeat, again, that those who ask their patron Saint for this kind of miracle or grace have a very poor conception of their Saint; that is, the conception of a Saint who intervenes to make an act of injustice in exchange of a gift or donation! But, as we have already stated, this is not the place for such argumentations. What we must now analyze are the social effects exerted by the widespread adoption of the *anti-legalistic and corrupting behavioral model*, mentioned above.

This corrupting model, arisen in the religious sphere, once it is acquired and becomes a mental habit, it is adopted by Catholics in the other spheres of human activity too, such as the social, economic and political spheres.

It should be underlined that such a corrupting behavioral model can be regarded as the underlying condition for the practice of the "recommendation", understood as an intervention of a powerful figure directed to obtain an illegal favor for the recommended person, in exchange for some compensation (money, allegiance, promise of a favorable vote, etc.). This has also been suggested by D. L. Zinn in his book *La raccomandazione — Clientelismo vecchio e nuovo* (2001).

However, we should once again make a distinction between apparently similar practices, which we could indicate with the terms "justified recommendation (or "introduction") and "illegal recommendation", to which we could add the "illegal imposition".

(1) The "justified recommendation" or "introduction", widespread in the Anglo-Saxon countries, contrarily to the "illegal recommendation" (see below) is not only lawful but also very useful and morally positive. It is characterized by the following features: the competence of he who recommends, a direct and specific relation between he who recommends and he who is recommended, the absence of any personal interest of he who recommends and his sincere conviction concerning the judgment that he expresses

about the person who is recommended. A typical example is that of a professor of Medicine who, at the end of a course (which entails a direct relationship between teacher and student), grants an evaluation of the ability and skillfulness of a student of his course by means of a "letter of introduction" or "letter of recommendation". This letter often has no definite addressee; it is usually addressed "To whom it may concern". A letter of introduction like this is *useful* to the recommended person because it allows him to assert for his career the true merits that he has shown; it is also morally positive because it helps the recommended person to be evaluated in the future in a truthful and just way.

(2) The "illegal recommendation" lacks all the features mentioned above, inasmuch as it is made by a person who is most often non-specifically competent to evaluate the specific merits of the recommended person and who has not had any direct and specific relationship with the recommended person but only relations of interest and/or friendship. A letter of "illegal recommendation" is usually addressed to a well-defined person

(typically "a friend", better if he is "power-ful"), most often a member of the organ legit-imated to judge, whose role is therefore rec-ognized and of which benevolence, indul-gence and "special" attention are invoked. The illegal recommendation is clearly di-rected to obtain something to which legally one is not entitled, and is therefore at the same time illegal and immoral. This kind of recommendation, made by the "influential persons" (on request by he who is interest-ed), is the one that corresponds, in the so-cial field, to what, in the religious sphere, is represented by miracles or graces granted by the patron Saints to their devotees who have turned to them by offering gifts and donations or some kind of "sacrifice".

(3) The "illegal imposition" not only lacks the features mentioned above (under point "*1*"), but is accomplished by a powerful per-son who, based on his power, imposes (overtly or under the appearance of respect-ing the legal form) his protégé or favorite, with the aggravating circumstance (in re-spect to the illegal recommendation) that the role of the organ legitimated to judge is compelled or even annulled, thus breaking

up the legal principles on which the function of the judging organ was based. The thinking and feeling underlying this kind of behavior might be as follows: if Saints favor their protégés, why should we, who are not Saints, not do the same? A typical example of illegal imposition may be the appointment of a head physician or surgeon by an "imposition" made by some politicians. This kind of recommendation, which sometimes is due to an initiative of a "powerful person" (who in this way wants to show and to increase his power), may be comparable to those happy events or cases of escaped danger that are *a posteriori* ascribed to the intervention of one's own patron Saint.

Of course, we should distinguish, on the one hand, the situations in which the appointments must be made, according to the laws, by politicians or by political organs (even if, in such cases too, appointments should be based on the merits of the aspirants); and on the other, the situations in which, according to the laws, appointment should be made by public competitions, carried out according to specified procedures, based on the evaluation of the ability and titles possessed by all aspirants (procedures that the undue pressure of politicians attempts to ignore or overthrow).

We could then affirm that: *justified recommendation* is useful, lawful and morally good; *illegal recommendation* is a more or less covert pressure on the correct application of the laws; whereas *illegal imposition* is an overt violation of the laws. Thus, both illegal recommendation and illegal imposition are at the same time illegal and immoral.

With reference to what occurs in Italy (as an example of what may happen in a typically Catholic society), I think it is useful to remember some norms of the Italian Constitution (see: Siclari 2007—but I would presume that similar statements are contained also in the Constitutions of other countries). Art. 3 establishes that "All citizens have equal social dignity and are *equal before the law*... It is the duty of the Republic to remove the obstacles... that... impede the *full development of the human person*". How can, a citizen, feel equal to others before the law if he is discriminated in favor of others who enjoy the support of the "powerful" persons? Moreover, how can, a citizen, attempt to realize the full development of his/her own person if the powerful figure of the moment, instead of removing the possible obstacles, adds the obstacle of his/her undue pressure? But there is a further article in the Italian Constitution that is even more specifically pertaining to the issue we are treating: "All citizens of either sex can access public offices and elective positions... under conditions of equality" (art. 51). The clarity of these articles does not allow any discussion or interpretation (*In claris not fit interpretatio*; that is, "What is clear cannot be the object of interpretation"). Moreover, art. 97 states that: "Public offices are organized according to the provisions of law, so as to ensure the efficiency and *impartiality of administration*". Hence, one could ask: how could the public administration be "impartial" if it favors certain citizens (the protégés of the "powerful" persons) at the expense of the others? Any democratic system requires that the access to public offices takes place according to the principles of equality and impartiality, and not according to particular interests or preferences. Thus, these largely accepted principles do not allow any escape for the cunning fellows; those who, abusing their power, attempt to impose their protégés cannot escape their responsibility.

However, apart from the distinctions made above, let us return to consider the many possible bad effects of what I named the *anti-legalistic and corrupting behavioral model*. Since the functioning of an entire society is based on the observance of its laws, a behavioral model consisting in ignoring rules and laws and in searching for the protection of the "powerful" figures leads to a diffusely corrupt society. Furthermore, I observe that the adhesion to the anti-legalistic and corrupting model is closely linked to the habit of illegality, which I discussed in chapter III; indeed, these are the two sides of the same coin.

It should also be underlined that the anti-legalistic and corrupting model, perhaps precisely because it arises in the religious domain, is adopted and even defended also by persons who, according to the common standard, would be regarded as "respectable people". I remember that many years ago, a senior colleague and friend of mine advised me: "Dear Francesco, one must have a Saint in Heaven in order to count for something in the academic world" (i.e., one must have the protection of some influential academic figure in order to count...). The utility or even the necessity of having "a Saint in Heaven" (that is, some powerful figure to turn to for favors) is experienced in all the spheres of the social life. It is associated to the conviction that, in practice, it is not the law that regulates human affairs but the will and influence of powerful figures, and that the powerful persons, if they can (and are not impeded by severe laws) act to defend their interests and the interests of their friends or protégés (instead of following the laws), in exchange for allegiance or other advantages. I remember what a close friend told me about a discussion among student candidates for a Master course in England. In discussing the procedure for admission, an Italian student worriedly observed: "But, surely this allows professors to make as many rigged choices as they like!"; to which, a Swedish student, rather astonished, answered: "Rigged choices? What a thing to say!". This episode clearly shows that the Italian student expected that professors, if they could, would decide incorrectly, by following their interests or preferences (granting favors in exchange for other favors) and not by following the rules (a possibility that he regarded as an exception), whereas the Swedish student, on the contrary, believed that the selection of the candidates would have occurred correctly (and regarded any incorrectness as a rare possibility).

The widespread adhesion to the *anti-legalistic and corrupting behavioral model* among Catholics favors the corruption of society, which becomes dominated by a *patronage system*. This phenomenon is present in all social classes, including both the low and the high classes, even if in the latter it acquires greater importance and visibility. Phenomena of patronage are often reported by the information media, but unfortunately restricted to the few cases that are discovered and furthermore with limitation, tacitly imposed by the patronage system itself.

Thus, in the academic world we have the phenomenon that, in Italy, is often indicated with the expression "university barony", but that in a more general manner may be defined as the prevalence of the allegiance to a "powerful professor" over the meritocracy. This means that the aspirant professor, if devoted to a powerful senior professor (that is, if he has "a Saint in Heaven"), will be helped to become himself a professor; he, then, from this new position, will reciprocate the favor that he has received. However, patronage, as I said, occurs at all levels in the academic world; it affects the assignation not only of the position of professors, but also of administrative positions and even those of porters.

In the high spheres of economy, patronage reigns over the assignment of managerial positions (in the board of directors or other high positions) in major enterprises as well as in the handling of biddings. Indeed, the shadow of patronage extends to the assignment of most of the biggest public and private contracts (in which high interests are at stake). Yet, once again, I underline that patronage influences even the assignment of minor positions and the biddings of medium or small magnitude.

In the political field, patronage finds a breeding ground for its flourishing. In a schematic way, we could say that it manifests itself by three mechanisms.

The *first* mechanism consists in the so-called "vote-buying", that is, in asking (or offering) votes in exchange for "favors" of various nature.

The *second* mechanism consists of the violation of the rules in force by "powerful" politicians or members of the public administration, in the sense that these people, instead of observing the rules and respecting the equality of the rights of citizens, grant "favors" to their protégés (in exchange for various rewards). This typically occurs in the carrying out of public biddings, but also in the many other acts of the public administration; in other words, the impartiality of the public administration (which in Italy, as in many other Western countries, is established by the Constitution) is often ignored.

The *third* mechanism consists in legislating (by parliament) and/or in administering public affairs (by the Executive) not in order to pursue the common good (as defined by the constitutional norms of the democratic States), but in order to satisfy the interests (or, more generally, the preferences) of individuals or groups "close" to some political party or powerful figures of the political or economic world. This mechanism, therefore, takes place at a higher level: not in the practical implementation of rules and laws, but in their definition and enactment by parliament or in their practical realization by the Executive.

It is of interest to note that the cult of Saints is present even in circles where nobody would expect to find it, such as the mafia circle. It is known, in fact, that several mafia members are devout to a patron Saint, from whom they expect, and to whom they ask, protection and favors. In other words, the mafia man, who is (or believes that he is) powerful (a power obtained by threatening and/or practicing violence) and, as such, grants favors and imposes his arrogance, himself turns to a powerful figure, more powerful than himself, his patron Saint, invoking protection and favors. The complex and intriguing phenomenon of the devotion of mafia men to Saints has been described and discussed in several publications, such as "*Il Signore sia con i boss*" ("The Lord be with bosses") by E. Mignosi (1993) and "*La Mafia Devota*" (The Devout Mafia) by A. Dino

(2008), to which the reader is referred for further information.

At this point, a reflection is in order: if the cult of Saints as patrons leads to a corrupt society, that is, a society in which many illegal actions occur, these actions should be checked, prevented and sanctioned by the Judiciary and the police. Therefore, one could ask: does a contrast exist between Judiciary and Police, on the one hand, and Catholics devout to Saints, on the other? To answer this question, we should consider the following.

Actions performed by citizens (men and women) cannot be distinguished in a sharp manner into legal and illegal. Moreover, some (perhaps many) illegal actions are not publicly demonstrable, that is, it is impossible to publicly demonstrate that they have occurred and/or that they are illegal.

Between legal and illegal actions, a grey zone of transition exists that comprises actions that are, so to say, "borderline". Let us suppose that in a public office there is an opening for promotion. The hypothetical director must select from among his personnel who should be promoted. This director publicly announces the interview day for the new opening, as prescribed by the law, as a working day with fifteen days notice. Let us say that the announcement is published on July 30, and the interview will be carried out on August 14. Only one candidate participates at the interview and passes the test. How should we judge the behavior of this director? On the one hand, this behavior appears perfectly legal. On the other hand, we should consider that the hypothetical director knew that, for long-lasting tradition, between July twenty and August 20 (period of peak summer heat in the hypothetical country to which we are referring) the work in the office decreases to the minimum and most employees are on holiday. Therefore, the announcement of the job opening, made on July 20, was not read by most of the interested people, which favors the few who could read the announcement. Based on the above, we could, at most, accuse the director of having been little wise for having fixed such an inappropriate date for the interviews; but lack of wisdom is not a crime and, therefore, it cannot be sanctioned by the Judiciary. Yet, it is possible that this director has followed the *anti-legalistic and corrupting behavioral model*, that is, has fixed these dates in such a way as to exclude some of the potentially interested people and to favor others. [Once again, the underlying self-justification of this director might be as follows: if Saints favor their protégés, at the expense of others, why can I not do the same myself?].

Concerning the *illegal actions publicly non-demonstrable*, they could be exemplified as follows. Let us suppose that the hypothetical director, mentioned above, in handling the interview for the promotion of the most deserving candidates, overtly violates the laws and rules, and favors the less deserving among the candidates. All the candidates (and all personnel) know the illegality made, so that the fact came to be known by the public prosecutor and the police. Consequently, an inquiry is open into these facts but, when the personnel is questioned by the public prosecutor (or by judges), all people deny what they have actually seen, i.e., the illegal acts performed by the director, because they fear the retaliation by the latter. Therefore, the prosecution must be dropped.

The above example shows the importance of a phenomenon which is often underrated (see my previous book—Belfiore 2011): the possibility of the *external conditioning* of the police, prosecutors, and judges, in the sense that the criminals who hold much power can prevent (or make difficult) the finding of the evidence of a given illegal action; or, conversely, they can facilitate the finding of evidence otherwise difficult to be found; or they can even provide false evidence (which may seem true). This in order to favor themselves, or their friends or their protégés, or in order to damage their rivals or enemies.

From the above, it is apparent that the Judiciary can only sanction those illegal actions that are evident or, in any way, publicly demonstrable. The instances of crime which are borderline or publicly indemonstrable escape the checking of the police, prosecutors and judges. To these instances, we should add those in which the responsible persons remain unknown. Yet, the actions openly illegal that are also publicly demonstrable are only a few in respect to: *(a)* the actions that are formally legal but are actually the result of the adoption of the *anti-legalistic and corrupting behavioral model*; *(b)* the actions openly illegal that remain unknown; *(c)* the known illegal actions of which the responsible persons remain unknown (this is true for the most instances of theft); and *(d)* the illegal actions that are publicly indemonstrable. This means that the laws, the police, the prosecutors and the Judiciary can punish only the minority of the instances of illegality that actually occur, whereas the majority of such instances remain unpunished. For the many cases that escape the checking of the law, the only possible remedy is represented by the sensibility of the community toward the respect of the laws. However, in a community in which there is a diffuse adhesion to the *anti-legalistic and corruptive behavioral model*, as in the Catholic community, pervaded with the cult of a patron Saint (and of the powerful Chief of the moment), it is precisely the sensibility toward the respect of the laws that is lacking or, at least, weak. Thus, a *vicious circle* takes place, inasmuch as the diffusion of the corrupting model prevents the rising of initiative against corruption in the com-

munity, and the lack of such initiatives favors the diffusion of the corrupting model.

Chapter VII—Outward Symbols of Power and Richness

Catholics are used to seeing the members of the ecclesiastic hierarchy, during the most significant religious events (like liturgical ceremonies), mantled by showy paraments, which strike their imagination as signs of great power and authority, of hierarchical distance from the common people. And the surroundings in which the members of the high ecclesiastic hierarchy live, and the magnificence with which they surround themselves, strengthen the impression of greatness and power. To this, the richness of personal ornaments (e.g., rings with precious stones) should be added, as well as the sumptuousness of their houses, apartments and rooms, the gold and the jewels that adorn certain statues of Saints or of the Virgin Mary, etc. All this confers to the high spheres of the ecclesiastic hierarchy, besides the appearance of *power*, also that of *richness*. Catholics, therefore, undergo a double influence. On the one hand, the Catholic Church formally preaches the praise of poverty and simplicity ("Blessed are the poor in spirit: for theirs is the kingdom of heaven", *Gospel of Matthew*, 5, 3) and of humility ("the last shall be first", *Gospel of Matthew* 20,16), and many priests of peripheral parish churches often bear witness to this. On the other hand, the high or major prelates, in their real and concrete life, show off striking signs of power and enjoy the benefit of richness. In other words, Catholics note that while, in theory, the simple ways of life that might be defined "humble" should be given prevalence, in practice external appearance and richness are preferred. And *form* is one thing; *substance* is another, different thing. This diversity between what is formally preached and what is practiced in the concrete life reminds us of the contrast between the laws that, in principle, should be obeyed and the habit of ignoring them in everyday life (see chapter III).

At this point, two explanatory arguments are required.

First, it is fully justified that the ministers of the Catholic Church bear external signs that make them recognizable by their believers, especially during liturgical ceremonies. What appears as questionable is the excessive showiness and sumptuousness of vestments, which conveys a sense of power and of hierarchical distance from the people of believers, especially the more humble. I think that it would be more appropriate to always wear simple garments, even during liturgical rites.

Second, considering the extent of the Catholic Church organization, it appears as necessary to have adequate economic resources, which may allow for the many activities that the Church carries out in the world. That is, it is right that the Church disposes of the economic means required to make its organization efficient. What appears as questionable is the enjoyment of richness (and the ensuing power) in a quantity that is beyond the functional requirement of the Church organization.

This stated, one has to note and to stress

the negative effects induced in the soul of Catholics by the ostentation of the insignia of the power and richness, which may prompt Catholics, even unconsciously, to search and to show off power and richness, to assign more weight to what one appears than to what one is, to pursue form instead of substance. Moreover, the contrast of this with the preaching, directed to inculcate disregard toward earthly things, like power and richness, and the appreciation of the Christian-Catholic virtues, ends up by inducing Catholics to hypocrisy: preaching virtue and practicing vice.

This *hypocrite behavioral model*, when interiorized by Catholics, manifests itself in various spheres of the social life.

The most typical examples are found in the field of politics (and also in that of economy), where any leader (that is, any figure that occupies an important political position) officially preaches civil virtues but informally (that is, in their concrete life) practices the vice of pursuing and showing off power and of practicing corruption, so often associated to power.

An additional negative consequence of

the adoption of the hypocrite behavioral model is exerted on the high clergy itself, which, being used to showing off power and richness, often ends up by appreciating those who in society are, and show to be, rich and powerful, and behave as such. Perhaps, these rich and powerful figures end up by being considered and respected more than the weak and humble people. Hence, the suspicion that the members of the high ecclesiastical hierarchy often may act as weak persons toward powerful people and as powerful persons toward weak people.

However, besides the powerful figures of the political and economic world (mentioned above), and perhaps the high prelates, it is society as a whole that is negatively affected by what I name the hypocrite behavioral model: to preach simplicity and distance from richness and to practice the pursuing and the showing off of power and money. We could ask ourselves: where are those Franciscan virtues of simplicity, humility and poverty?

Chapter VIII—Pseudo-Values and Pseudo-Disvalues

As the title of this chapter shows, the Catholic world is characterized by the pursuing of false values or *pseudo-values* and by the condemnation of false disvalues or *pseudo-disvalues*.

Of the pseudo-values pursued by Catholics, it suffices to mention *chastity*, the *fear of God*, and the observance of some *precepts of the Church*.

With regard to *chastity*, or "purity", it should be underlined that the population of Catholics is obsessed by anything that concerns sex. Practicing a normal sexual activity, instead of being considered the expression of a healthy personality, is regarded as something sinful and immoral, based on the conviction that the practice of a normal sexuality is a synonym of sin. The pseudo-virtue of chastity is held in great regard, up to overwhelming any other positive quality of the human person, especially as far as women are concerned. Therefore, it may happen that, in judging a woman, only a minor value is assigned to her intelligence, sensibility, honesty, etc., because what is regarded as really important is whether she is, or not, *chaste*. It may happen, then, that a woman who is dull-minded, shabby, insensible, wretched, envious and yet chaste is preferred to a woman who is intelligent, open-minded, sensible, generous, with an affectionate nature but who has had sexual experience (of course, here we refer to serious sexual experiences, expression of serious feelings). The cult of the disvalue "chastity" and the condemnation of any sexual experience (except those between a married couple and directed to procreation) constitute the essential characteristics of a behavioral model that might be defined as *sex-phobic behavioral model*. This explains the condemnation of homosexuality by Catholics, since any sexual act of homosexuals is obviously *not* directed to procreation. The severe consequences of the adoption of the sex-phobic model are well known, and include the oppression of women, some cases of the so-called crimes committed for motives of "honor", the sense of guilt inculcated especially in the soul of the most ingenuous persons, etc.

The pseudo-value of chastity may be regarded as belonging to a large class or category of pseudo-values, which includes the *observance of the precepts* of the Catholic Church, observance that is based on the *fear of God*. Those who observe such precepts are named God fearing persons. These people observe the Ten Commandments (most of which are to be absolutely accepted) as well as the five precepts of the Catholic Church, and they regard any inobservance of any of such precepts as deadly sins. These precepts, among others, include the command "to attend Mass on Sundays and other holy days of obligation" (*Compendium of the Catechism of the Catholic Church*, §432), whose infringement constitutes a "mortal sin".

Thus, for Catholics, he who does not attend Mass on Sunday and/or does not "confess his or her mortal sins *at least* once a year" (*Compendium of the Catechism of the Catholic Church*, §305) commits a mortal sin and should be condemned to the eternal fire of hell! What an absurdity!

The assignment of importance to such absurd and insubstantial pseudo-values, and the ensuing upsetting of the hierarchy or priority of the values have far-reaching consequences, which affect the entire society and its organization.

As far as *pseudo-disvalues* are concerned, they can be regarded as the symmetrical opposite of pseudo-values: impurity, an inobservance of Church precepts, some "sins" regarded as such by the Catholic doctrine, as having divorced, having had an abortion or having given one's assent to an abortion (other "sins" are justly recognized as disvalues by most Western democracies).

The pursuing of values and the condemnation of disvalues that are not actually such have a close relationship with the recognition of absurd rules treated in chapter III, because the absurd rules are exactly those rules that command the pursuing of disvalues and the shunning of false disvalues. The acceptance of such an absurd conception of values and disvalues can be regarded as the adhesion to a *disvalue-pursuing behavioral model* that, as all deviant behavioral models, leads to serious consequences in all aspects of social life. To confirm this, several examples can be given, including: *(a)* the numerous instances of "honor killing" ("crimes for reasons of honor"); *(b)* when people do not resort to crime to avenge some "offense to the honor", the feelings of hatred and enmity and the ensuing behaviors; *(c)* the alienation and the tacit condemnation of persons who are actually innocent; and *(d)* the recognition of merits to persons who do not deserve them; etc.

It is worth noting that some of the absurd "rules" whose inobservance constitutes sin for Catholics would be acceptable if they were conceived as something symbolic. Thus, the precept of "to attend Mass on Sundays" (see above) would be acceptable (indeed, it would have a great meaning) if it were understood as a warning directed to every man and woman to remind them that, even if the majority of their lives can be devoted to pursue egoistic ends (i.e. earthly things or material goods), there should be at least some days (Sundays) during which they should think about spiritual things, that is, ethical issues and the moral sense of life, because this makes human beings more responsible for themselves and others, and more aware of their nature and their destiny. If, instead, as it actually occurs, all this is reduced to the imposition of a rigid rule or a strict formalism (to attend Mass on Sundays), the result is that a correct warning is converted into an absurd pretension.

Chapter IX—Religion and Politics

Religion should be distinguished from politics, and the Church from the State (laity of the State), because in a democratic State there must be the possibility that several different religions co-exist pacifically. However, sometimes a contrast may arise between the precepts of a religion, defended and promoted by the upholders or guardians of it (i.e., the members of the ecclesiastical hierarchy), and the prescriptions of the laws enacted by the parliament. This is because a religion can be regarded as a general conception of life and the world, a comprehensive doctrine, based on faith (and not on reason, as the philosophical conceptions of the world are) which, as such, also includes precepts of moral nature and hence binding for its "believers". And so, a contrast between the religious precepts and the laws of the State may arise.

Let us briefly examine the conditions under which such a contrast may occur (see also my previous book—Belfiore 2011).

When religious precepts and the prescriptions of the laws are in agreement (either in commanding or in prohibiting some actions), there cannot obviously be any contrast.

Conversely, when religious precepts prohibit what the laws prescribe, contrast is unavoidable. For instance, if in a given country with a high rate of population growth the laws prescribe that it is forbidden to have more than two children, and that, if further pregnancies occur, parents *must* resort to abortion or face punishment; and if the dominant religion in this hypothetical country considers abortion as a "mortal sin", then a contrast is unavoidable. This is also true in the instances in which the religious precepts prescribe what the laws of the State prohibit. In these situations, a solution could be found if the citizen is able to distinguish his *private* moral conception (to which he adheres as *individual* or *person*) from the *public* moral conception, imposed by the State by its laws (to which he adheres as *a citizen*). Yet, such a distinction is not easy to be accepted or easy to be realized.

On the other hand, when religious precepts prohibit what the laws of the State allow (that is, what the laws do not punish), no contrast should arise. This is the case of abortion as regulated by the laws in most Western countries, in which the law allows abortion, even if within certain temporal limits and under certain conditions. The reason why in these instances there should be no contrast is that any female citizen is *free* to follow the precepts of her religion, which prohibit her to abort, or not to follow the precepts of religion and to have an abortion. Yet, concerning the laws on abortion (and on other actions prohibited by religion but *allowed* by the State), the Catholic ecclesiastic hierarchy exerts an active propaganda against the enactment of such laws. This is incomprehensible and unjustified, because the State does not exert any pressure on the conscience of the believers, who remain free and can freely choose to follow, or not to follow, the dictates of their religion. If we think about this, it becomes apparent that the pretension of the Catholic ecclesiastic hierarchy to obtain that the laws prohibit what religion prohibits means to pretend to impose the observance of religious precepts by means of police, which would be an unworthy pretension. What meaning, from the religious standpoint, could the observance of religious precepts have if imposed by the law? Obviously, none.

From the standpoint of my discourse, we could say that the problem arises from the fact that Catholic people receive and, so to say, suffer the pretension of the ecclesiastic hierarchies, and take into account, in their political choices, the unjustified claims of the Church, which could certainly be defined as undue interferences in the sphere of politics. It is evident that in the countries where there is a large preponderance of Catholics (e.g., Italy, where, in addition, the Vatican is located), the interference of the Church suffered by Catholics leads to a severe distortion of the free political activity of society.

What has been said above concerning abortion could be repeated for other practices prohibited by the Church but allowed by the State, such as the possibility to practice *divorce*. In these instances too, the State does not impose by laws a given behavior, but it leaves citizens free to choose, based on their religious (or, more generally, moral) convictions and feelings, how to act. Yet, in the countries where there is a preponderance of Catholics, the legislation on divorce, in order to be implemented, has required a difficult work of conviction in order to contrast the active propaganda and the interference by the Church. The undue interference of the Catholic ecclesiastic hierarchy in the political sphere drives many Catholics toward political intolerance, that is, prompts them to adopt an *intolerant behavioral model*.

From the above, it is apparent that Catholics, by suffering the interference of the claims of the Church, do not succeed in distinguishing the sphere of religion from that of politics. However, it is true that the mixture of religion and politics is even more pronounced in the populations that follow other religions (e.g., Islam); nonetheless, the fact remains that it should be regarded as an undue and unjustified mixture.

Chapter X—Catholicism: Cause or Effect?

In the preceding chapters, I attempted to draw a picture of the negative effects that Catholicism, as understood and received by the majority of Catholics, exerts on the private and public life in the societies in which it represents the predominant religion.

In the various chapters, I have discussed separately some aspects of the doctrine and of the precepts (in a broad sense) of Catholicism, and I have indicated, for each of such aspects, the kind of negative behavioral model that is favored or induced. If we now attempt to put together the various aspects that we have discussed, that is, if we attempt to make a synthesis of all the consequences of Catholicism, what results is a very negative and complex behavioral model, which summarizes the various behavioral models that I have mentioned in the various chapters; that is, an *authoritarian, superstitious and miracle-based, anti-legalistic, immoral, male-chauvinist, corrupting, hypocrite, sex-phobic, disvalue-pursuing and intolerant behavioral model.* Shortly, this can be named the *Catholic behavioral model.*

It is then quite evident that the adoption of such an anomalous behavioral model should necessarily lead to a corrupt and disordered society and, consequently, culturally underdeveloped and economically little evolved. It should be added that Catholicism (as any religion) is a very special factor in respect to other factors that may affect the beliefs, feelings and hence the behavior of human beings, such as, for instance, school education. In fact, as it has been said, the effects of school education are received only during the first stage of life, and therefore they may be later attenuated or corrected by learning from the experiences of life and from the reflection on the ethical principles and values that should be followed. Catholicism, instead, as any other religion, once it is endorsed, will exert its influence for a lifetime, from childhood to death.

At this point, however, we should ask ourselves a fundamental question: is the adhesion to Catholicism the cause or the effect of the *authoritarian, superstitious and miracle-based, anti-legalistic, immoral, male-chauvinist, corrupting, hypocrite, sex-phobic, disvalue-pursuing and intolerant behavior* that has been described in the preceding chapters? In other words, is it the adhesion to Catholicism that produces such a behavior or is it the natural aptitude toward this behavior that leads to the adhesion to Catholicism? The answer to such a question is not simple. I think, however, that the issue raised by this question is an aspect of the wider problem concerning whether human behavior is mainly determined by endogenous factors (that is, to natural endowment) or to external-environmental factors (i.e., cultural, religious, economic, or other factors). Even if it is clear that such a complex problem cannot be discussed here, not even in a concise manner, I think that we could assume as a very probable hypothesis that human behavior results from the combined effects of both endogenous and exogenous factors, and that the uncertainties and the related debates concern the different "weight" that is assigned to each of the two factors. Indeed, I think that the "weight" of these two factors may vary from person to person, linked to the characteristics of the various personalities: the personality whom, in a simple way, we could define as "strong" will be less affected by the exogenous or environmental factors, whereas the personality whom we could define as "weak" will be much affected by such factors. For the sake of simplicity, we could hypothesize that, on average, both kinds of factors contribute to the human behavior to an equal extent, that is, each to the extent of 50%. Based on this, we should briefly consider the role of the endogenous or genetic factors and that of the exogenous or environmental factors in determining the behavior of the Catholic people, which we have described in the preceding chapters. It should be specified, however, that the factor "Catholicism" is one of the various exogenous-environmental factors that determine human behavior. Hence, instead of considering the contrast "environmental factors" versus "genetic factors", we should consider the contrast "Catholicism" versus "other environmental factors + genetic factors"; for the scope of our discourse, we could name the latter term as "extra-catholic factors".

The role of the *extra-catholic factors* seems to be suggested by the fact that some typical characteristics of the behavior of Catholics, such as the cult of Saints, are much more profoundly felt and diffusely practiced by Catholics of certain geographic areas (South-Europe, Latin America) in respect to other areas (North-Europe, North-America). On the other hand, the role of Catholicism is also suggested by the observation that among the inhabitants of a given geographic area, Catholics show a behavior that differs from the one of the non-Catholics as far as the characteristics described in the preceding chapters are concerned. To keep faith with the simple nature of this book, I cannot further discuss this complex issue, which, however, has been debated for a long time. Here I just mention the thesis defended by the Swiss Protestant (of Italian origin) J.C.L. Simonde de Sismondi in the volume XVI of his *Histoire des Républiques*

Italiennes du Moyen Age (1809-1818), who, in particular on pages 413-433, maintains that the Catholic Church has exerted negative effects on the morality of Italians. As it is known, this thesis was refuted by A. Manzoni (1819) in his "*A Vindication of Catholic Morality*", where he, on page 1, referring to the Catholic moral system, affirms that "this system is the only holy and reasonable one, and that corruption arises from not understanding it, from disobeying it, or from misunderstanding it, and that it is impossible to find any one valid argument against it: ...". Perhaps, both theses contain a part of the truth. Or, better, perhaps Manzoni referred to Catholicism as conceived and felt by a great spirit, such as himself, whereas Sismondi referred to Catholicism as conceived and felt by the large majority of Catholics (Italian and non-Italian); that is, by the 95% of Catholics to whom I myself refer in this book.

This stated, it seems of interest to attempt to understand what the characteristics of the "extra-catholic factors" that favor the adhesion to Catholicism and, hence, the adoption of the *Catholic behavioral model* are. It is useful, to this end, to compare the characteristics of the populations of the geographical areas that are typically Catholic, as are those of Italy and Spain, and the characteristics of the predominantly non-Catholic populations, such as those of Great Britain and North-Europe.

The typically-Catholic populations often show a preference for a kind of morality that could be defined "private morality"; this is a morality that has as its end or scope the good of the persons with whom one has a direct and enduring relationship, that is, a morality that is more valid in the sphere of the family members, relatives, friends and perhaps acquaintances. This at the expense of what could be defined as "public morality", based on the observance of rules and laws equal to all. Such a moral conception manifests itself by several of the characteristics present among the Catholic populations. On this ground, it is possible to understand the profound sense of the affective bonds that link family members, relatives, and friends. This is shown, for instance, by the often unbelievable sacrifices undergone by parents to help their children (e.g., to support their education, up to a university degree, or even further), and the strong wish to favor one's friends, even at the expense of violating the laws that define the public morality (the latter is felt as something abstract and distant). The same meaning should be assigned to the strong sense of hospitality felt toward friends and even acquaintances.

Conversely, the predominantly non-Catholic populations show a preference for the "public morality", as defined by the norms, laws, and rules enacted by democratic institutions. This kind of morality, then, is more attentive to the observance of the "rules" which, by their proper nature, possess the characteristics of generality; that is, they are equal for all, and do not allow particular or special treatments prompted by the feelings of affective relationship or friendship or common interests. This kind of morality helps to explain the weakness of the affective bindings among family members and relatives. This is indicated by the fact that young people, once they become of age, often leave home to live a totally independent life. Furthermore, parents tend not to feel obliged to help and sustain their children after they become of age (this is a fact that certainly favors the development of the sense of responsibility and the growth and maturity of the human person). The same meaning should be ascribed to the treatment given to friends and acquaintances, always marked by respect but also characterized by some distance and coldness.

In conclusion, by keeping faith to the criterion of extreme simplicity adopted in this book, we could schematically envisage that Catholicism prompts or favors the aptitude (genetic or acquired) to give more "weight" to the "private morality" in respect to "public morality", which means to privilege the affective interpersonal relationships in respect to those impersonal relationships as regulated by the laws. It is evident that the better solution is to integrate the two kinds of morality that, when correctly understood, do not exclude each other but rather appear as the two components of a general conception of morality that include both of them.

I hope that the reflection on what has been briefly treated in this book may help Catholics to come out from the closed limits of the private morality and to endorse the principles and values of a moral conception that includes both the "private" as well as the "public" spheres of human life.

Appendix: Why Religion?

In the preceding chapters, I have briefly described the "negative" effects of Catholicism. Yet, in the Introduction of this book I underlined that the negative consequences that, in my opinion, are exercised by Catholicism as perceived by the masses are not sole of Catholicism, as other branches of Christianity and other religions may be the cause of similar or different negative consequences. Therefore, a fundamental question arises: If religions have some negative consequences, how could it be explained that all people of the world, in all times, have professed some form of religion and have believed in the dogmatic truths that all forms of religion impose to their followers? Indeed, one could endorse the view of several thinkers, like B. Russell who stated that "What the world needs is not dogma, but an attitude of scientific inquiry" (1957: 165). However, the practically universal spread of the religious attitude among human beings suggests that this phenomenon must be due to some fundamental underlying reason. The nature of this book, characterized by brevity and simplicity, prevents a full discussion of this complex issue. Therefore, I will limit myself to the following elementary considerations.

It should be understood that human beings have the insuppressible aspiration to give meaning to their life and to have a conception of what the world as a whole is. A tiny minority of people may rely on their "attitude of scientific inquiry" (to use Russell's words, mentioned above), and they attempt to attain a philosophical conception of the world that is coherent and rational; that is, they attempt to elaborate the most general (or supreme) hypothesis about reality for which some support by observational data and/or rational deduction is possible. They are content with what can be obtained by human reason, and are neutral about the possible (indemonstrable) hypotheses concerning what remains unknown. Conversely, most people do not possess an "attitude to scientific inquiry" or, simpler, do not have a rational mentality; rather, as I noted elsewhere (Belfiore 2007, p. 158), they are driven by their profound desire (indeed, a true need of the soul) to give some answer to the fundamental questions about human fate and the interpretation of the whole universe, so that they end by believing by faith in some indemonstrable hypotheses, which actually are imaginary tales, commonly called religions. The latter, therefore, are collective creations made by human intellect through its imaginative ability, under the emotional stimuli proper of human soul. In other words, religion might be defined as elementary and romanticized philosophy of the masses. Thus, the desire to know the origin of the universe and of life is satisfied by imagining that there is a God, who created all things in the universe; the strong desire to survive death prompts to believe in the immortality of the soul; the aspiration to know what is good and what is bad is gratified by resorting to what God has established; the wish of justice leads to believe that, after death, God will judge us according to divine and, therefore, just criteria; and so on. For these reasons, contrary to the assertion of Russell, mentioned above, that "What the world needs is not dogma, but an attitude of scientific inquiry", we could affirm that the large majority of human beings (excepted the tiny class of intellectuals engaged in human sciences) do not have "an attitude of scientific inquiry" and, consequently, they need exactly a set of "dogmas" (no matter whether irrational and unjustified) that provide them with some kind of worldview, and indicate to them some "moral" values and the ensuing norms of conduct.

For all these motives, religion, with all related beliefs and feelings and the ensuing laws and rules, will always be present in all societies made of human beings.

Once again, I wish to note that believing in God is a respectable mental position; what is criticizable is the way in which most people conceive God and the religion, which includes many particular imaginary beliefs to "explain" the many unknown aspects of the observed universe and to fulfill the innumerable aspirations of the human soul.

Essential Bibliography

Belfiore, Francesco (2007). *The Ontological Foundation of Ethics, Politics, and Law*. Lanham, MD: University Press of America.

Belfiore, Francesco (2011). *The Democratic Society and Its Founding Concepts*. Lanham, MD: University Press of America.

Benedetto XVI (2010). *Luce del mondo* (una conversazione con Peter Seewald). Roma: Libreria Editrice Vaticana.

Catholic Church (2005). *Compendium of the Catechism of the Catholic Church*. United States Conference of Catholic Bishops. [see also: http://www.vatican.va/archive/compendium_ccc/documents/archive_2005_compendium-ccc_en.html]

Constitution of the Italian Republic. Rome: Senato della Repubblica. [See also: http://www.senato.it/documenti/repository/istituzione/costituzione_inglese.pdf]

Dino, Alessandra (2008). *La Mafia Devota. Chie-*

sa, Religione, Cosa Nostra. Roma-Bari: Later-
za.

Gospel of Matthew. See: http://www.earlychri-
stianwritings.com/text/matthew-kjv.html

Manzoni, Alessandro [1840-42]. *The Betrothed*,
translated by Bruce Penman. New York: Pen-
guin, 2004.

Manzoni, Alexander [1819]. *A Vindication of
Catholic Morality*. London: Keating and
Brown, 1836.

Merriam-Webster's Dictionary and Thesaurus.
Merriam Webster, 2006.

Mignosi, Enzo (1993). *Il signore sia coi boss. Sto-
rie di preti fedeli alla mafia e di padrini timo-
rosi di Dio*. Palermo: Arbor.

Mill, John Stuart [1861]. "Considerations on
Representative Government", in *On Liberty
and Other Essays*, edited by John Gray. New
York: Oxford University Press, 1998.

Pius IX (1870). *Decrees of the First Vatican Coun-
cil ("Aeterni Patris")*. (see: Papal Encyclicals
Online.   http://www.papalencyclicals.net/-
Councils/ecum20.htm).

Powell, Mark E. (2009). Papal Infallibility: A
Protestant Evaluation of an Ecumenical Is-
sue. Grand Rapids, MI: William B. Eerdmans
Publishing.

Russell, Bertrand [1957]. *Why I am Not a Christian*. London: Routledge, 2004, p. 165.

Siclari, Massimo (2007). *La costituzione della*

Repubblica italiana nel testo vigente. Roma: Aracne.

Sismondi De, J. C. L. Simonde [1809–1818]. *Histoire des Républiques Italiennes du Moyen Age*, Tome seizième. Paris: Treuttel et Wuertz, 1826.

Tanner, Norman P. (editor) (1990). *Decrees of the Ecumenical Councils*, 2 Volume Set. Georgetown University Press.

United Nations [1948]. *Universal Declaration of Human Rights: Dignity and Justice for All of Us*. 60th Anniversary Special Edition 1948-2008. United Nations, 2008.

Zinn, Dorothy L. (2001). *La raccomandazione - Clientelismo vecchio e nuovo*. Roma: Donzelli.

Index

Index